Wild Animals

Patricia Walsh

Illustrations by David Westerfield

Heinemann Library
Chicago, Illinois

Customer Service 888-454-2279
Visit our website at www.heinemannraintree.com

Designed by Kimberly Miracle and Q2A Creative
Illustrated by David Westerfield
Photos by Kim Saar, p. 4; Mark Ferry, p. 5
Printed in China by WKT

10 09 08 07 06
10 9 8 7 6 5 4 3 2 1

New edition ISBNs: 1-4034-8925-4 (hardcover)
                   1-4034-8932-7 (paperback)

The Library of Congress has cataloged the first edition as follows:
Walsh, Patricia, 1951-
      Wild Animals / by Patricia Walsh ; illustrations by David Westerfield.
         p. cm. – (Draw It!)
      Includes bibliographical references and index.
Summary: Presents instructions for drawing twelve different kinds of wild animals, including an elephant, a monkey, a panda, and a toucan.
ISBN 1-57572-351-4 (lib. bdg.)
1. Animals in art – Juvenile literature. 2. Drawing – Technique – Juvenile literature.
[1. Animals in art. 2. Drawing – Technique.] I. Westerfield, David, 1956-ill. II. Title.

NC780 .W35 2001
743.6 – dc21
                                    00025761

Acknowledgments
Cover photograph reproduced with permission of Royalty-Free/Getty.

Every effort has been made to contact copyright holders of any material reproduced in this book. Any omissions will be rectified in subsequent printings if notice is given to the publisher.

Disclaimer
All the Internet addresses (URLs) given in this book were valid at the time of going to press. However, due to the dynamic nature of the Internet, some addresses may have changed, or sites may have changed or ceased to exist since publication. While the author and publisher regret any inconvenience this may cause readers, no responsibility for any such changes can be accepted by either the author or the publisher.

Some words are shown in bold, **like this**. You can find out what they mean by looking in the glossary.

Contents

Introduction

Would you like to improve the pictures that you draw? Well, you can! In this book, the artist has drawn pictures of wild animals. He has used lines and shapes to draw each picture in small, simple steps. Follow these steps and your picture will come together.

Here is advice from the artist:

- Always draw lightly at first.
- Draw all the shapes and pieces in the right places.
- Pay attention to the spaces between the lines as well as the lines themselves.
- Add details and **shading** to finish your drawing.
- And finally, erase the lines you don't need.

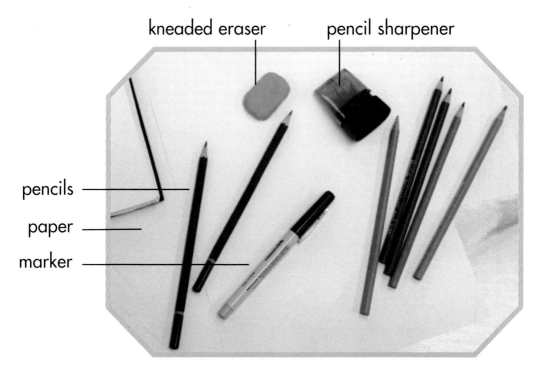

You only need a few supplies to get started.

There are just a few things you need for drawing:

- a pencil (medium or soft). You might also use a fine marker or pen to finish your drawing.

- a pencil sharpener

- paper

- an eraser. A **kneaded eraser** works best. It can be squeezed into small or odd shapes. This eraser can also make pencil lines lighter without erasing them.

Now are you ready? Do you have everything? Then turn the page and let's draw!

The drawings in this book were done by David Westerfield. David started drawing when he was very young. In college, he studied drawing and painting. Now he is a **commercial artist** who owns his own graphic design business. He has two children, and he likes to draw with them. David's advice to anyone who hopes to become an artist is, "Practice, practice, practice—and learn as much as you can from other artists."

Anteater

The giant anteater lives in tropical forests and grassy plains from Mexico to Argentina. It eats ants and termites by poking its long, sticky tongue into their nests and licking them up.

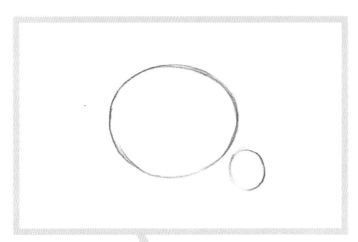

Step 1:

Sketch a large circle for the body and a small circle next to it for the head.

Step 2:

Draw two lines to connect the head and the body. Make a swooping curved line to begin the tail.

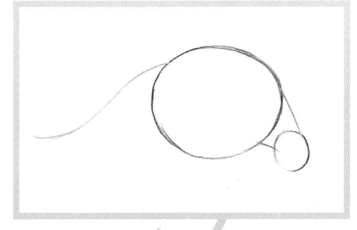

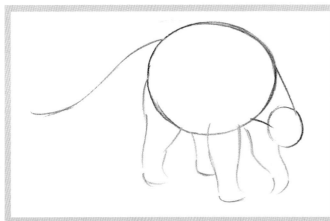

Step 3:

Draw four thick legs under the large circle. Start the top of the legs at the lower edge of the big oval. Gently curve the leg lines downward. Round off the ends for feet. Draw the front feet pointed and turned in.

Step 4:

Add the anteater's long **snout** to the small circle. Then erase the bottom of the small circle to make a long, narrow head. Add a large dot for an eye. Draw two small leaf shapes for ears. Draw a long, skinny tongue at the end of the snout.

Step 5:

Shape the underside of the tail with a curved line. Use long pencil strokes to make the tail bushy. Use short squiggly lines to add a furry edge to the belly and legs. Draw a double set of lines on the body that look like a wiggly V.

Step 6:

Draw sharp claws on the ends of the front feet. Draw a shorter claw on the front edge of the back foot. **Shade** a band of black hair from the throat to the middle of the back. Leave a white border on either side of the black band. Shade in the rest of the anteater. Finish by drawing a rounded ant hill in front of the anteater.

Bison

Bison are also called buffalo. Large herds of bison once roamed the Great Plains of North America. Some of today's highways follow the same routes once used by bison herds.

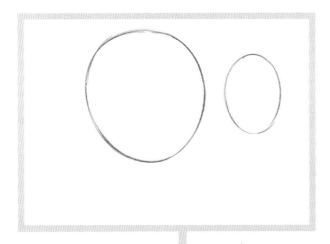

Step 1:

Sketch a large oval and a small oval next to each other.

Step 2:

Draw a small overlapping circle on the larger oval for the head. Draw a rectangular shape below it for the **snout**. Connect the first two ovals at the top and bottom.

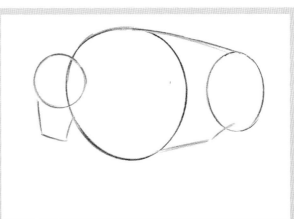

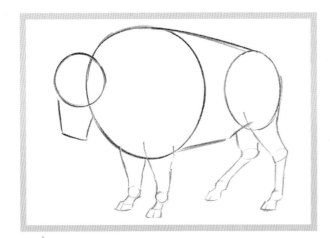

Step 3:

Draw two front legs below the large oval. Draw two back legs below the small oval. Make the legs thicker at the top and narrower at the feet. Square off the ends for hoofs. Draw small circles on the legs to position the ankles and knees.

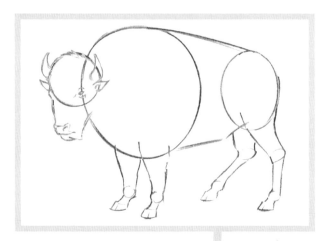

Step 4:

Draw a pointed horn on each side of the head. Draw two small pointed ears below the horns. Add a dark pointed oval for an eye. Only one eye can be seen in this picture. On the snout, draw a butterfly shape for the nose and a line below for the mouth.

Step 5:

Use squiggly lines to make the bison's shaggy beard, chest, shoulders, and front legs. The **hindquarters** have shorter hair, so those lines are smooth. Add the short, thin tail with long hair on the end.

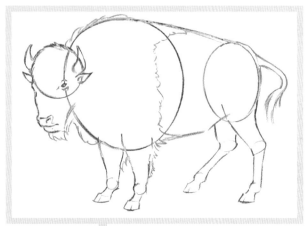

Step 6:

Erase the oval and circle **guidelines**. Use **shading** around the head, neck, shoulders, and under the legs to show the bison's heavy fur. Use light pencil strokes to make the tall prairie grass near its feet.

Elephant

The Asian elephant is one of the largest land animals. Asian elephants live on the tropical grassy plains and in the forests of Asia. An elephant can use the end of its trunk to examine and hold small objects.

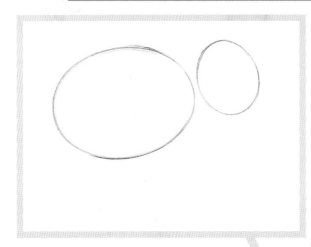

Step 1:

Lightly **sketch** two ovals side-by-side for **guidelines**. The larger oval will be the body.

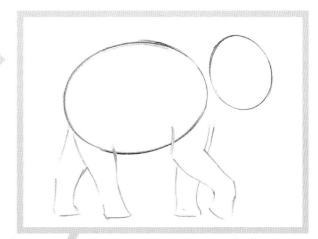

Step 2:

Draw four legs under the larger oval. Draw the legs so they are almost as wide at the top as they are at the bottom. Square off the bottoms for the feet.

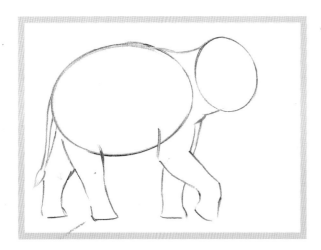

Step 3:

Draw a line across the top of the ovals to connect the head and body. This line should go all the way to the elephant's left rear leg to form the top part of a tail. Add a shorter line and connect the two with a pointed shape at the end. Draw a curved line to connect the head to the front leg.

Step 4:

Add the elephant's long trunk to the small oval. Reshape the head so it has a bump at the top and a lower lip below the trunk. For a male elephant, add long pointed **tusks** to either side of the trunk. Add an eye. Sketch short lines around the eye. Erase the guidelines.

Step 5:

Draw a leaf-shaped ear at the back of the head. Add a few more short lines below the eye to give the head shape.

Step 6:

Finish by drawing half circles on each foot for toenails. Sketch short lines across the trunk. Then **shade** some parts of the head, the inside of the legs, and a big shadow under the elephant.

Giraffe

The giraffe is the tallest of all animals. Giraffes live on the grassland south of Africa's Sahara Desert. Their long legs and long neck help them eat leaves from the tops of trees.

Step 1:

Lightly **sketch** two ovals side by side for **guidelines**. Make the second oval a bit larger.

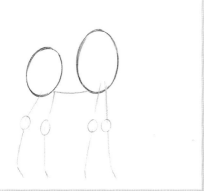

Step 2:

Connect the two ovals with a curved line. Begin the legs by drawing four long lines. Draw two lines coming from the first oval and two from the second oval. About halfway on each line, make a circle for the knee. Make a short, curved line to connect the two oval shapes.

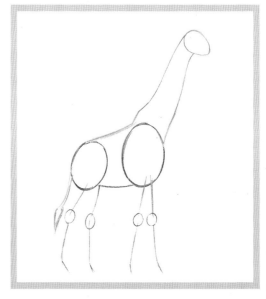

Step 3:

Draw a small oval above the larger oval for the head. Draw it as far above the oval as the feet are below the oval. Connect the head to the larger oval with two long lines. Add a sloping line to connect the tops of the first two ovals. Add a ropelike tail. Put a **tuft** of hair on the end.

Step 4:

Finish the long, thin legs. Start the lines at the body and draw a line on either side of each circle knee. End each leg with a **wedge**-shaped hoof.

Step 5:

On top of the head, draw two short horns. Add two pointed ears. Draw an oval eye in the center of the head. Reshape the end of the head into a narrow **snout**. On the end of the snout, add a short line for a mouth and a large dot for a nostril.

Step 6:

Erase the guidelines. Darken the important lines. Use very short pencil strokes to add a narrow, dark **mane** to the neck. Draw the pattern of spots. Use **shading** to darken the spots. Leave white spaces around each one.

Lion

Lions are large, roaring cats. Today they live mostly in protected areas south of Africa's Sahara Desert and in a wildlife **sanctuary** in India. The male lion's neck and shoulders are encircled by a great hairy **mane**.

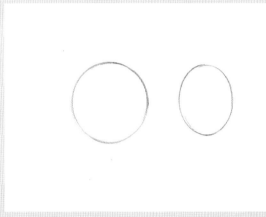

Step 1:

Sketch a large circle and a smaller oval next to each other. These are your **guidelines**.

Step 2:

Sketch a circle above and to the side of the larger circle. To this circle add a box-shaped **snout** with a notch for the mouth. Draw lines to connect the tops and bottoms of the oval and circles.

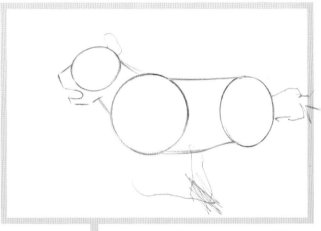

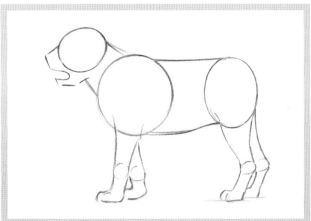

Step 3:

Draw short, thick legs, two under the circle and two under the oval. End each leg with large rounded feet. Sketch a circle in the middle of each leg to make knees.

Step 4:

Make the long, thin tail with two swooping curved lines. End the tail in a **tuft** of hair.

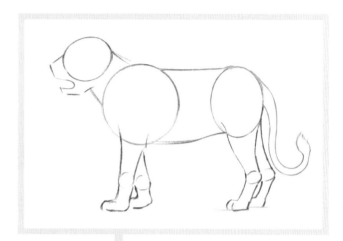

Step 5:

Draw a half circle for an ear. Lightly **shade** a curved line inside the ear. Add an oval eye and make a few short pencil strokes in front of it. Draw a triangle on the end of the snout for a nose. Draw tiny triangles inside the mouth for teeth. Sketch a rough mane from chin to legs and from head to shoulders.

Step 6:

Erase the guidelines. Use squiggly pencil strokes to fluff the mane and tail tip. Darken the important lines and add shading under the lion's body.

Monkey

The rhesus monkey is also called a macaque. It lives on rocky hillsides and in forests, temples, and villages in southeast Asia. Rhesus monkeys eat insects and fruit.

Step 1:

Lightly **sketch** two **guideline** ovals above a branch. Make the branch by drawing a thick V lying on its side.

Step 2:

Connect the ovals with a long curving line. Continue the curving line below the branch. Then draw a long tail wrapped around the branch.

Step 3:

Draw a circle for the head next to the first oval. Add a smaller, overlapping circle for the **snout**. Draw two legs under the first oval. Sketch a short line between the two ovals. Draw the third and fourth legs.

Step 4:

Darken the line between the bottoms of the two first ovals with a squiggly line. Draw curving fingers or hands to make the monkey look as if it is grasping the branch.

Step 5:

Begin the face by making a rounded M shape a little way down on the head. Under the M add two black circles for eyes. Add a half circle to each side of the head for ears. Shape the snout, then add dots for nostrils and a short line for a mouth. Draw a squiggly line from the snout to the top of the front leg.

Step 6:

Erase the guidelines. **Shade** in the rhesus monkey with long, soft pencil strokes to give it a silky coat. Darken the area on the top of the head, under the tail, and on the back legs.

Moose

The moose is the largest American deer. It lives in the forests of the northern Rocky Mountains, along the Canadian border, and in northern New England. Moose have long legs so they can run fast and walk in deep snow.

Step 1:

Lightly **sketch guidelines** for a circle and two overlapping ovals.

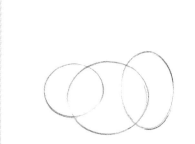

Step 2:

Draw a smooth line to connect the tops of the circle and ovals. Draw the front legs by making an X. Make stick shapes for each of the back legs. Connect the stick shapes with circles. These are for the knees and the ankles. Add one large circle and two smaller ones to the X shape.

Step 3:

Begin the head with a circle and a small oval. Connect them to each other and to the big oval with short, straight lines. Add a curved line on the side of the small oval to make a big upper lip.

Step 4:

Begin the leg lines at your circle and oval guidelines. Draw a line on either side of each circle knee. End each leg with a heart-shaped hoof. Begin to shape the moose's chest with a curved line coming from the front legs.

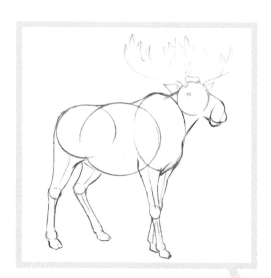

Step 5:

To draw the moose's **antlers**, begin with a curved line on top of its head. Then draw sharp points above the line. Add a small oval eye. Draw two leaf-shaped ears below the antlers on either side of the head.

Step 6:

Draw a comma-shaped nostril on the **snout**. Use a curving line under the head to add a long flap of skin called the bell. Make short, light pencil strokes to **shade** in hair. Shade the inside of the legs darker. Shade the antlers and a shadow under the feet. Use light pencil strokes to sketch in grass.

Panda

The giant panda lives in bamboo forests in central China. Bamboo is the pandas' main food. There are far fewer pandas today than in the past because people have moved into their **habitats**.

Step 1:

Draw a triangle with rounded corners. Draw a circle on top of the triangle. These are your **guidelines**.

Step 2:

Use a wavy line to smooth the shape between the circle and the triangle. Draw two thick legs near the bottom of the triangle. Draw two more legs near the middle of the triangle. Draw an oval at the end of each leg.

Step 3:

Make the circle for the head wider. Draw a short, curved line to shape the **snout**. Add long, small ovals on top of the head for ears.

Step 4:

Add tiny ovals for eyes. Draw a circle around each eye. Draw a curved line with a tiny triangle at the end for a nose. Add a little wavy line under the nose for the mouth. In the panda's right paw, draw a long, thin bamboo **shoot** with a few leaves on one end.

Step 5:

Erase the guidelines and make the outlines bolder. Make a few pencil strokes in the ears and around the head and legs to show the fur. Pandas have short tails, but this panda's tail can't be seen.

Step 6:

Use **shading** to darken the patches around the eyes. Shade the nose, ears, legs, and chest. Also make a dark band across the shoulders. **Sketch** short, straight lines around the panda to show bamboo.

Tiger

The tiger is a very large and powerful cat. Tigers live in forests, swamps, and grasslands in Russia, China, India, and other parts of Asia.

Step 1:

Lightly **sketch** two ovals side by side. These are your **guidelines**.

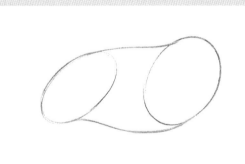

Step 2:

Connect the tops and bottoms of the ovals with curved lines for the back and belly.

Step 3:

Draw a circle next to the oval on the right. Add half of a wide oval to the side of the circle. This begins the **snout**. Make a shape like a thick J on the oval at the left for the tail.

Step 4:

Draw four legs along the underside. Begin each leg at the guidelines. Make the legs thick. Draw a small circle near the middle of each leg for the knee. End each leg with an oval to make the paw. Add a few short lines on each paw for toes.

Step 5:

Smooth the lines that connect the big ovals and the head circle. Add pointed ovals to the top of the head for ears. Draw a dot inside a circle for the eye on this side of the head. Reshape the snout, and add a tiny triangle for the nose and a wavy line for the mouth.

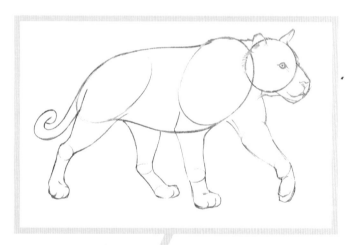

Step 6:

Erase the guidelines. Draw the tiger's stripes by making thick, short lines up and down on the body and side to side on the legs. Add some stripes on the face. Draw some dots and a few short whiskers on the snout. Add **shading** under the body. Sketch short, straight lines for grass.

Toucan

The toucan is a noisy bird with a loud call. It lives in the tropical forests of South America. Toucans eat fruit, insects, and lizards.

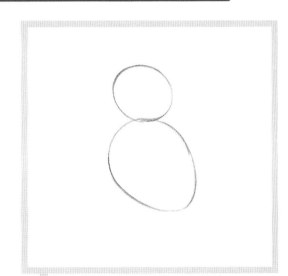

Step 1:

Lightly draw a small tilted oval with a larger egg-shaped oval below. These are your **guidelines**.

Step 2:

Draw two **parallel** lines ending in a V below the guidelines for a branch. Then draw two legs between the larger oval and the branch. Draw four fingerlike toes wrapped around the branch. Only the front toes can be seen here.

Step 3:

Connect the head and body with two short curved lines. Add a long banana-shaped beak to the front of the circle. Begin the beak as wide as the circle. Shape it like a large, curving W.

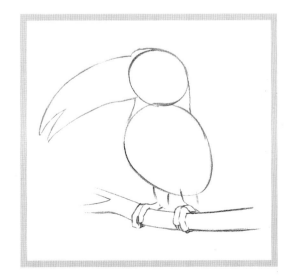

Step 4:

Draw the wing as a flattened, pointed oval along the toucan's back. Draw a large rounded oval below the wing for the tail. You cannot see all of the tail because some of it is behind the branch.

Step 5:

Make the lines of the beak darker. Add a few lines of **shading** on the beak. Behind the beak, add a large dark dot inside a circle. Show the area of light feathers by drawing a squiggly line from the eye to the middle of the body and across the chest.

Step 6:

Draw a few straight lines on the tail and wing to show the big feathers. Then shade between these lines. Darken the body with the side of your pencil and shade a pattern on the beak. Leave a pear-shaped area blank on the front of the toucan's body, or make it a lighter color.

Wolf

The wolf is the largest wild dog. The gray wolf is also called a timber wolf. It is nearly **extinct** in most of the United States, but still lives in Alaska, Canada, and Russia.

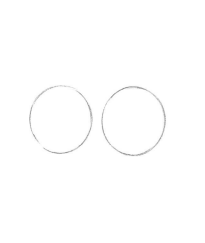

Step 1:

Sketch two same-sized circles side by side for your **guidelines**.

Step 2:

Draw a smaller circle for the head above the second circle. Connect the tops and bottoms of all the circles with curving lines.

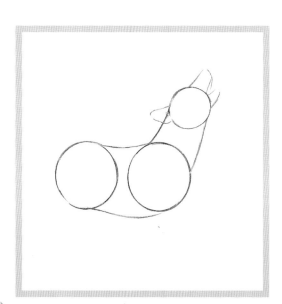

Step 3:

Draw a shape near the top of the head circle that is nearly square. This is for the **snout**. Make a V-shaped notch in the snout for the mouth. Add a rounded triangle shape to the side of the head for the ear.

Step 4:

Draw two legs coming from each body circle. Start each leg at the bottom of the guidelines. Make the legs wider near the body and narrower at the feet. Use straighter lines for the front legs than for the back legs. Add circles halfway down the back legs. Make circles near the bottom of the front legs.

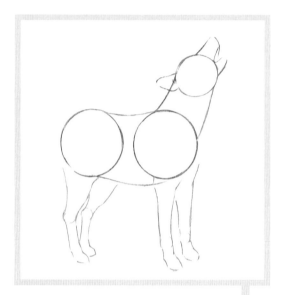

Step 5:

Add two curved lines that meet in a point for the tail. Add some **shading** inside the ear. Make a dot for the eye near the top of the head and a dot on the end of the snout for a nostril. Use short pencil strokes along the outline to give the wolf a furry coat.

Step 6:

Erase the guidelines. Add shading behind the head, ears, tail, and on the left rear leg. Shade in a shadow underneath the wolf.

Zebra

Zebras live in herds on the grassy plains and mountains of eastern, central, and southern Africa. There are fewer zebras than there used to be because they were once hunted for their striped skins.

Step 1:

Sketch two circles side by side to make your **guidelines**.

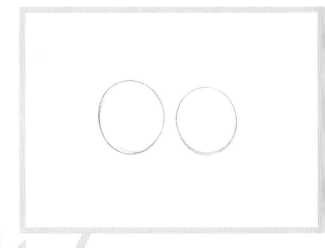

Step 2:

Draw a smaller circle for the head above and to the side of the second circle. Add an even smaller circle below the head for the nose. Connect the tops and bottoms of all the circles with curved lines.

Step 3:

Draw two V shapes under the first circle for the back legs. Sketch a V shape and a straight line under the second circle for the front legs. Draw circles for the knees at the points of the Vs and halfway down the straight line. Add two curved lines that meet at a point for the tail.

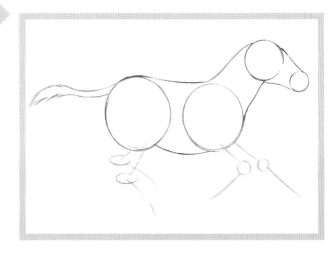

Step 4:

Begin the leg lines at the bottom of the circle guidelines. Draw a line on either side of each circle knee. Make a **wedge**-shaped hoof at the end of each leg. Draw the far back leg so it can only be partly seen.

Step 5:

Draw a tiny C for the nostril on the end of the nose. Make a short, curved line for the mouth. Draw a small pointed oval for the eye. Add a pointed leaf-shaped ear to the top of the head. Use a squiggly line along the top of the neck to make the zebra's **mane**.

Step 6:

Darken the outlines. Erase the guidelines. Draw wide stripes toward the rear and narrow stripes toward the front of the zebra's body. Draw stripes on its legs, neck, and head. Then **shade** in every other stripe. Sketch short lines under the zebra for grass.

Glossary

antler hornlike growth on the head of some animals

commercial artist person who designs and illustrates things for other people

extinct no longer alive

habitat place where an animal naturally lives

hindquarter rear part of an animal's body

mane thick hair that grows on the neck of an animal

sanctuary place where something is protected

shoot new growth of a plant

snout part of an animal's head that has the nose, mouth, and jaws

tuft bunch of hair

tusk long, pointed tooth that sticks out

Art Glossary

guideline
light line used to shape a drawing. This line is usually erased in the final drawing.

kneaded eraser
soft, squeezable eraser used to soften dark pencil lines

parallel
straight lines that lie next to one another, but never touch

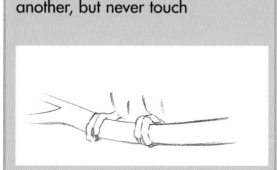

shade
make darker than the rest

sketch
draw quickly and roughly

wedge
shape with sloping sides that tapers to a thin edge

Find Out More

Books

Claybourne, Anna. *Giant Panda.* Chicago: Heinemann Library, 2005.

Lee, Justin. *How to Draw Animals of the Rain Forest.* New York: PowerKids Press, 2002.

Spilsbury, Louise, and Richard Spilsbury. *A Herd of Elephants.* Chicago: Heinemann Library, 2004.

Waters, Jo. *The Wild Side of Pet Cats.* Chicago: Raintree, 2005.

Websites

National Zoological Park
http://nationalzoo.si.edu

Index